Not Like the Others

Emily Peluso

Pixelated Publishing
:: Buford, Georgia ::

This is a Lil' Digital Book
by

An Imprint of
©2019 Faithful Publishing
All Rights Reserved
ISBN: 978-1-940911-13-7

Character Design – Emily Peluso and Keaton Pascoe
Art Director – April S. Fields

We dedicate this book to:

Mom & Dad who always believe in me – Emily Peluso

All those who dare to be different. – A. S. Fields

Table of Contents

There are all sorts of reasons to be 'not like the others' but if you just do you to the best of your ability you will always be exactly enough.
~ Meema

4

Lilybird sits in a tall Sycamore tree on the very tip top branch. She likes it there because she can see.

She can see the big sky and the far away horizon.

She can see everything that happens on the ground below.

She can see the others playing and doing what they do.

6

She can see Malcombird chasing Marybird and Missybird, like he always does. She knows it's just a game but she thinks it might be a little bit silly.

She can see Mandybird and Mindybird sharing secrets and laughing, like they always do. She knows they like to talk about the others but she thinks it might be a little bit mean.

She can see Miltonbird and Macbird fighting over a worm like they always do. She knows it's just the way they like to play tough and they are really best friends.

She can see Mollybird, Masonbird, and Mischabird practicing their chirping for the upcoming big test.

Lilybird dreads the test because she cannot chirp like the others but she doesn't know why.

She looks like the others, she is very good at many things, but she can't chirp like the others so she never chirps in hopes that no one will notice.

And while all the others are doing what they do, to keep her secret, Lilybird prefers to sit alone in the tall Sycamore tree high up on the tip top branch.

When Mizbird comes out and tweets that recess is over
all the others flitter and flutter back into class.

In class, Mizbird quiets the others down so they can begin.
As usual Lilybird is already quiet.

Mizbird announces it is time for their final big test of
their chirping skills.

Everyone takes a turn and then it's time for Lilybird to chirp. She knows it isn't going to end well but she sees no way out. She decides she has to try her best anyway.

She stands up as tall as she can and opens her little beak and then belts out a noise that sounds sort of like a fog horn.

For what seems like the longest minute in the history
of ever, the others stare in shock...

And then they start laughing...

...and then Macbird falls
over he is laughing so hard.

Lilybird is so embarrassed she flies away as fast as she can.

. . .back to the tip top branch of the Sycamore tree where she plans to stay for at least a million years.

. . .or at least until it's time to go back home.

At the end of the school day the others flitter and flurry out of class. Lilybird knows they are still laughing about her and her very loud chirp.

And they are, but mostly they are happy to be out of school too.

And so they are not paying attention.

But where Lilybird sits, she can see what the others don't. She can see Hungry Hawk soaring above the forest floor where the others are too busy to notice.

Lilybird does not think twice. She fills her little chest and belts out a warning chirp that sounds like a very loud fog horn.

The others, startled, look up to see Lilybird in the tip top of the Sycamore tree honking and flapping her wings. . . and Hungry Hawk diving down towards them.

In one big flurry of feathers the others run for cover. Hungry Hawk just misses grabbing up Miltonbird and after circling around a couple times must go somewhere else to find his dinner.

When the coast is clear, the others and Mizbird come out
and call to Lilybird to
"Come down!
Come down!
Come down!"

Lilybird sighs then spreads out her little wings and floats
back to the others so she can be humiliated some more
. . . she thinks.

When she lands, the others all gather round her making so much noise no one can understand anything. Mizbird quiets them down and says, "Lilybird, you are our hero! Thank you! Thank you! Thank you!"

20

Lilybird sits high in her Sycamore tree but now she sits with great purpose, doing what she does best. She looks out to the big sky and far away horizon and sees all good things ahead.

For the first time ever, she is super glad to know that everyone is different in some ways and, more importantly, that it's okay she is not like the others.

An Interview With Emily Peluso

Q: So, Emily, when did you learn that you have dyslexia?

Em: I was ten, last year, in fourth grade.

Q: What was it like for you in school before you were diagnosed?

Em: I struggled. I could not spell or read. I was reading at kindergarten level in fourth grade. I felt discouraged all the time. I didn't understand why it was so hard.

Q: Were there any classes for you to help you with your difficulties?

Em: Well, no, they put me in a special needs class because my school didn't know how to work with dyslexia. Basically I didn't learn much in fourth grade, because they thought I was unteachable, so, yeah, they did not help me. But I think a new law was just passed in Georgia though that will help make people understand dyslexia better.

Q: At the end of fourth grade was when your parents decided to do home-school and enroll you in Orton-Gillingham, a special tutoring program for dyslexia. So, where are you now at the end of fifth grade?

Em: I'm now reading at fifth grade level because I have been working hard and I've had a lot of help from different people. Plus now I feel so much better about myself too.

Q: What advice would you give a kid who is struggling with reading but doesn't know why?

Em: Don't give up! Don't feel dumb. Figure out what you are good at because everyone has weaknesses. Know that, if you do have dyslexia, you are not alone, and it's just that your brain is wired differently. And pay no attention to bullies who try to make fun of you or try to make you feel dumb. Who cares what they think? Many very successful people are dyslexic.

A Parent's View

We are the parents of a dyslexic child. WOW! After the initial confusion of the diagnosis wore off, we learned how to become advocates for our daughter. We decided to home school our daughter and explore private tutoring. During her time of homeschooling, Emily brainstormed the idea of writing a book about the struggles of dyslexia with her much loved "Meema". And this beautiful book is the result.

Our hope for other families is to provide resources for when you feel helpless, hopeless and frustrated. It will be okay and there is help available. Educate yourselves by reading evidenced-based information about dyslexia and most importantly … BREATHE! You've got this. There are so many resources and support groups available in this information overloaded world.

The most critical decision we made was finding a Certified Dyslexia Practitioner with the IDA (International Dyslexia Association). Our wonderful, amazing, life changing tutor is certified at the Associate level through the Academy of Orton-Gillingham Practitioners and Educators (AOGPE). O-G tutoring for us has been the ticket to aiding Emily in crossing the reading bridge. We cannot brag on or thank her enough for what she has done for Emily.

Some Important Takeaways

Talk openly with your child about learning differences. Make life fun...we say "Leprechauns took off with that memory file...maybe they will return it tomorrow". Your child is not stupid in any manner and there is help available. Use the word dyslexia, sometimes repeatedly (______ is dyslexic, has dyslexia or with dyslexia...there is no wrong way).

Ask for clarification when needed, especially during IEP meetings where the educational system seems to speak a different language. Don't sign anything at meetings - take it home and reread and digest it. Don't be afraid to ask questions and you will have many. Your pediatric provider can be a great resource. Ask them for guidance. Most importantly, love your dyslexic child, they have so very much to offer by how they see the world much like Lilybird! Tap into their superpower, whether it is art, physical ability with sports, music, science, engineering or the vast array that makes up our great kiddos!

So go advocate for your child...or better yet, teach them to advocate for themselves!

David & Janet Peluso

About Dyslexia
Jessica R. Northcutt

What is dyslexia? The Yale Center for Creativity and Dyslexia describes dyslexia as an unexpected difficulty in reading in an individual who has the intelligence to be a much better reader.

Sally Shaywitz says dyslexia is complex. It requires our brains to connect letters to sounds, put those sounds in the right order, and pull the words together into sentences and paragraphs we can read and comprehend. People with dyslexia have trouble matching the letters they see on the page with the sounds those letters and combinations of letters make. And when they have trouble with that step, all the other steps are harder.

Dyslexic children and adults struggle to read fluently, spell words correctly and learn a second language, among other challenges. But these difficulties have no connection to their overall intelligence. While people with dyslexia are slow readers, they often, paradoxically, are very fast and creative thinkers with strong reasoning abilities.

Dyslexia is also very common, affecting 20 percent of the population and representing 80– 90 percent of all those with learning disabilities. Scientific research shows differences in brain connectivity between dyslexic and typical reading children, providing a neurological basis for why reading fluently is a struggle for those with dyslexia.

Dyslexia can't be "cured" – it is lifelong. But with the right supports, dyslexic individuals can become highly successful students and adults.

Orton-Gillingham (O-G) is an instructional approach intended primarily for use with individuals who have difficulty with reading, spelling, and writing of the sort associated with dyslexia. It is practiced as an approach, not a method, program, system, or technique. In the hands of a well-trained and experienced O-G practitioner, it is a powerful and life changing tool.

The Orton-Gillingham approach has been used since the 1930's. O-G is the only scientifically proven method to remediate dyslexia and other language learning differences. The approach is named after Samuel T. Orton and Anna Gillingham. Samuel Orton (1879-1948) was a neuropsychiatrist and pathologist. Anna Gillingham (1878-1963) was a gifted educator and psychologist with a superb mastery of the language. Together, they created the Orton-Gillingham approach.

An Orton-Gillingham lesson is always focused on the learning needs of the individual student. Students with dyslexia need to master the same basic knowledge about language, and its relationship to our writing system, as any who seek to become competent readers and writers. However, because of their dyslexia, they need more help sorting, recognizing, and organizing the raw materials of language for thinking and use. Language elements that non-dyslexic learners acquire easily must be taught directly and systematically.

The Academy of Orton-Gillingham Practitioners and Educators describes the following principles that make up the Orton-Gillingham approach.

Personalized
Teaching begins with recognizing the differing needs of learners. While those with dyslexia share similarities, there are differences in their language needs. In addition individuals with dyslexia may possess additional problems that complicate learning. Most common among these are attention deficit disorder (ADD) or attention deficit disorder with hyperactivity (ADHD).

Multisensory
It uses all the learning pathways: seeing, hearing, feeling, and awareness of motion, brought together by the thinking brain. The instructor engages in multisensory teaching to convey curricular content in the most understandable way to the student. The teacher also models how the student, by using these multiple pathways, can engage in multisensory learning that results in greater ease and success in learning.

Diagnostic and Prescriptive
An Orton-Gillingham lesson is both diagnostic and prescriptive. It is diagnostic in the sense that the instructor continuously monitors the verbal, nonverbal, and written responses of the student to identify and analyze both the student's

problems and progress. This information is the basis of planning the next lesson. That lesson is prescriptive in the sense that will contain instructional elements that focus upon the resolution of the student's difficulties and that build upon the student's progress noted in the previous lesson.

Direct Instruction
The teacher presentations employ lesson formats which ensure that the student approaches the learning experience understanding what is to be learned, why it is to be learned, and how it is to be learned.

Systematic Phonics
It uses systematic phonics, stressing the alphabetic principle in the initial stages of reading development. It takes advantage of the sound/symbol relationships inherent in the alphabetic system of writing. Spoken words are made up of individual speech sounds, and the letters of written words graphically represent those speech sounds.

Applied Linguistics
It draws upon applied linguistics not only in the initial decoding and encoding stages of reading and writing but in more advanced stages dealing with syllabic, morphemic, syntactic, semantic, and grammatic structures of language and our writing system. At all times the Orton-Gillingham Approach involves the student in integrative practices that involve reading, spelling, and writing together.

Linguistic Competence
It increases linguistic competence by stressing language patterns that determine word order and sentence structure and the meaning of words and phrases. It moves beyond this to recognizing the various forms that characterize the common literary forms employed by writers.

Systematic and Structured
The teacher presents information in an ordered way that indicates the relationship between the material taught and past material taught. Curricular content unfolds in linguistically logical ways which facilitates student learning and progress. Sequential, Incremental, and Cumulative

Step by step learners move from the simple, well-learned material to that which is more and more complex. They move from one step to the next as they master each level of language skills.

Continuous Feedback and Positive Reinforcement
The approach provides for a close teacher-student relationship that builds self-confidence based on success.

Cognitive Approach
Students understand the reasons for what they are learning and for the learning strategies they are employing. Confidence is gained as they gain in their ability to apply newly gained knowledge about and knowledge how to develop their skills with reading, spelling, and writing.

Emotionally Sound
Students' feelings about themselves and about learning are vital. Teaching is directed toward providing the experience of success. With success comes increased self-confidence and motivation.

Jessica R. Northcutt
~Dyslexia Specialist~
www.myogtutor.com
https://m.facebook.com/dyslexiaogtutor/

Jessica R. Northcutt
~Dyslexia Remediation~
www.myogtutor.com
Founder/Owner Georgia Orton-Gillingham Tutoring
Certified Dyslexia Practitioner/IDA
Associate/AOGPE

Orton-Gillingham Tutors
Specializing in Reading, Spelling, Writing, Math and Phonological Awareness

For More Information

Some of the resources we have found helpful:

www.dyslexiaida.org. International Dyslexia Association

www.madebydyslexia.org
Sir Richard Branson affiliated with this website. So many GREAT resources- fact sheets to give teachers, great easy to understand informational text called "connecting the dots".

www.understood.org

www.dyslexia.yale.edu

www.wrightslaw.com
Great books including "Wrightslaw: From Emotions to Advocacy: The Special Education Survival Guide" ...a must read for advocating effectively for your child.

Must read books:

Fish in a Tree by Lynda Mullaly Hunt

The Dyslexic Advantage by Brock I. Eide

Overcoming Dyslexia by SallyShaywitz, M.D.

Facebook pages to check out:

International Dyslexia Association

Decoding Dyslexia (some states have their own page)

Made by Dyslexia (all time fav)

Georgia Orton-Gillingham Tutoring